1

I0489918

Table of Content

Introduction

In recent years, the rise of the internet and digital technology has revolutionized the way we work and earn money. With the flexibility and convenience of working from home online, it's never been easier to achieve financial freedom and independence. Whether you're a stay-at-home parent, a digital nomad, or simply looking for a way to supplement your income, the opportunities for making money online are endless. In this book, we will explore ten proven strategies for earning up to $10,000 per month from the comfort of your own home.

The key to success in the online world is finding a niche that aligns with your passions and expertise, building a strong personal brand, and providing value to your audience. By creating valuable content, building an email list, and promoting affiliate products, you can generate a significant income stream.

Additionally, creating and selling digital products, starting a dropshipping business, offering consulting services, and freelancing are all viable options for building a profitable online business. Finally, investing in stocks and cryptocurrency can be an excellent way to grow your wealth and achieve long-term financial security.

While there is no guarantee of success, by following the strategies outlined in this book and putting in consistent effort and dedication, you can build a thriving online business and achieve financial freedom. So let's get started on the journey towards earning up to $10,000 per month from home online!

Chapter 1: Identify your Niche

Identifying your niche is the first and most important step toward building a successful online business. Choosing a niche that aligns with your interests and expertise will not only make it more enjoyable to work on your business but also help you establish credibility and authority in your industry. In this chapter, we will discuss the importance of identifying your passion and talents, researching profitable niches, and selecting a niche that aligns with your interests and expertise. By the end of this chapter, you will have a clear understanding of how to choose a niche that you are passionate about and that has the potential to be profitable.

1. Identifying your passion and talents:

Identifying your passion and talents is an essential first step in building a successful online business. Your passion is what will drive you to put in the hard work and dedication necessary to succeed, and your talents will help you provide value to your audience. When you choose a niche that aligns with your passions and expertise, you're more likely to create content that resonates with your audience and establishes you as an authority in your industry.

To identify your passion and talents, start by brainstorming your interests and hobbies. What topics do you enjoy reading about or discussing with others? What activities do you spend your free time on? It's important to choose a niche that you genuinely enjoy, as this will make it more enjoyable to create content and engage with your audience.

Next, consider your skills and expertise. What topics do you have experience in or knowledge about? What are some of your professional strengths? Choosing a niche that aligns with your skills and expertise will help you create content that is informative and valuable to your audience. Once you have a list of potential niches, research them further to determine their potential profitability. Look for niches where there is high demand and where customers are willing to pay a premium price for products or services. You can use tools like Google Trends and social media analytics to identify trends and popular topics in your niche.

It's important to note that your niche doesn't have to be unique or groundbreaking. It's often better to choose a niche that has some competition, as this indicates that there is already a market for your products or services. However, it's important to differentiate yourself from your competitors by providing unique value and building a strong personal brand.

In summary, identifying your passion and talents is a crucial first step in building a successful online business. By choosing a niche that aligns with your interests and expertise, you can create content that resonates with your audience and establishes you as an authority in your industry. Take the time to research potential niches and evaluate their profitability, and remember to differentiate yourself from your competitors by providing unique value and building a strong personal brand.

2. Researching profitable niches:

Researching profitable niches is an essential step in starting an online business. While it's important to follow your passions and interests, not all niches can be profitable. Therefore, it's important to evaluate the market and see if there is a viable audience for your niche. You should start by analyzing the competition and determining how much demand there is for your product or service. Understanding your target market and identifying their needs and pain points is also essential. It's also important to evaluate the potential profit margins for your business, as well as the costs of producing or sourcing your product. Conducting thorough research can help you determine whether your niche has the potential to be profitable in the long run. This will allow you to make informed decisions and create a sustainable and successful online business.

Here are some tips on how to research profitable niches:

- **Start by identifying broad topics:**

  To begin researching profitable niches, it's essential to identify broad topics that interest you or align with your expertise. You can start by brainstorming a list of topics that you enjoy or are knowledgeable about. Once you have a list of potential niches, it's important to conduct research to determine which ones are most profitable. You can use tools like Google Trends and Keyword Planner to identify the search volume and competition for keywords related to your niche. You can also analyze your competitors' websites and social media profiles to determine which niches are most popular and have growth potential.

  Once you have identified a profitable niche, it's important to research your target audience thoroughly. This involves understanding their needs, pain points, and preferences. You can use social media analytics tools to determine which platforms your target audience uses most frequently and what types of content they engage with. You can also conduct surveys or focus groups to gather more in-depth information about their needs and preferences. Additionally, analyzing your competitors' customer base can provide valuable insights into what types of products or services are most popular within your niche. By keeping up with the latest trends and continually refining your strategies, you can provide the best possible value to your customers and build a successful online business.

- **Use keyword research tools:**

Keyword research tools are invaluable for identifying popular search terms in your chosen niche. These tools allow you to see the number of searches for specific keywords and phrases, as well as the level of competition for each term. By analyzing these metrics, you can get an idea of the level of demand for products or services related to your chosen niche.

For example, if you are interested in starting a blog about healthy eating, keyword research tools can help you identify popular search terms related to that topic, such as "healthy recipes," "meal planning," or "nutrition tips."

You can use this information to create content that is optimized for search engines and tailored to the interests and needs of your target audience.

Additionally, keyword research tools can help you discover long-tail keywords, which are longer, more specific phrases that are less competitive but may have higher conversion rates. By incorporating these keywords into your content, you can attract more targeted traffic to your website and increase your chances of converting visitors into customers or subscribers.

- **Analyze online trends:**

Another way to analyze online trends is to monitor social media platforms and online forums related to your niche. This can help you identify the conversations, questions, and concerns that your target audience is having in real-time. By monitoring these channels, you can gain valuable insights into the pain points and challenges that your audience is facing, which can inform the content, products, and services you create. Additionally, you can participate in these conversations to establish yourself as a thought leader and build relationships with potential customers.

It's important to note that while analyzing online trends can help identify profitable niches and create content that resonates with your target audience, it's not the only factor to consider. It's important to also evaluate the competition in your niche, the potential profitability of your business idea, and your skills and expertise in the field. By conducting thorough research and analysis, you can increase your chances of building a successful and profitable online business.

- **Check bestseller lists:**
  In addition to analyzing bestseller lists on online marketplaces, it's also important to pay attention to bestseller lists and rankings within your specific niche. For example, if you're interested in the gardening niche, you might want to look at bestseller lists for gardening books or tools. This can give you a better understanding of the types of products that are

popular within your niche and help you identify opportunities for your own business. You can also use this information to stay up-to-date with industry trends and to monitor the competition.

It's worth noting that while bestseller lists can provide valuable insights, they should not be the only factor you consider when researching profitable niches. It's important to also analyze customer demographics, competition, and overall market trends to get a comprehensive understanding of your target audience and the potential profitability of your chosen niche. By combining data from various sources, you can make informed decisions about the products or services you offer and increase your chances of building a successful online business.

- **Analyze social media engagement:**

Analyzing social media engagement is a dynamic and ongoing process that requires regular monitoring and refinement. By tracking engagement metrics over time, you can identify patterns and trends that can inform your content strategy and help you make data-driven decisions about your online business. For example, you might notice that your audience is more engaged with video content than written content, or that certain topics consistently generate more engagement than others. Armed with this knowledge, you can adjust your content strategy to focus on the types of content that are most likely to resonate with your audience.

In addition to analyzing engagement metrics, it's important to actively engage with your audience on social media. This includes responding to comments, thanking followers for their support, and asking for feedback on your products or services. By engaging with your audience in this way, you can build a sense of community around your brand and establish a relationship of trust with your customers. This can ultimately lead to increased brand loyalty and advocacy, as satisfied customers share their positive experiences with others.

Finally, social media engagement can also be used to test and refine your marketing strategies. By experimenting with different types of content, messaging, and promotions, you can see which strategies are most effective at driving engagement and ultimately sales. This can help you optimize your marketing efforts and improve your ROI over time.

- **Evaluate competition:**

Evaluating competition is a crucial step in researching profitable niches. By analyzing your competitors' websites, social media profiles, and marketing strategies, you can gain insights into what is already working in your niche and identify gaps in the market that you can fill. Take note of their offerings, pricing, and messaging to understand their unique value proposition and what sets them apart from other competitors. This information can help you identify opportunities for differentiation and create a competitive advantage for your online business. It's also important to analyze your competitors' customer base to understand their target audience and what resonates with them. Look at customer reviews, social media engagement, and demographic data to identify patterns and preferences. Use this information to create content and products that address the specific needs and pain points of your target audience. Additionally, analyzing your competitors' marketing strategies can help you identify gaps in their approach that you can capitalize on. Look for ways to create more engaging and effective marketing campaigns that appeal to your target audience.

Finally, while it's important to analyze your competitors, it's also important to focus on building your brand and unique value proposition. Use the insights you gain from your competition analysis to create a differentiated and compelling brand identity that resonates with your target audience. Focus on providing unique value and creating a memorable customer experience that sets you apart from your competitors. By striking a balance between analyzing your competitors and building your brand, you can create a sustainable and profitable online business in your chosen niche.

In summary, researching profitable niches is essential to building a successful online business. By using keyword research tools, analyzing online trends, checking bestseller lists, evaluating social media engagement, and analyzing competition, you can identify niches that have high demand and profitability potential. Remember to choose a niche that aligns with your interests and expertise and to differentiate yourself from your competitors by providing unique value and building a strong personal brand.

3. Selecting a niche that aligns with your interests and expertise:

Choosing a niche that aligns with your interests and expertise is essential for building a successful and sustainable online business. When you work in a field that you are passionate about, it becomes more than just a job; it becomes a fulfilling and enjoyable experience. By combining your interests with your business, you can create content, products, and services that are authentic and resonate with your target audience, which can help you attract and retain customers.

Additionally, your expertise in your chosen niche can give you a competitive edge and position you as a thought leader in your industry. Ultimately, choosing a niche that aligns with your interests and expertise can lead to greater success and fulfillment in your online business endeavors.

Here are some tips on how to evaluate a niche based on your interests and expertise:

- **Choose a niche that aligns with your interests:**

  When you are passionate about a topic, you are more likely to stay up to date with the latest news, trends, and developments in the field. This knowledge and enthusiasm can help you create high-quality content and offer valuable products or services to your audience. Additionally, when you enjoy the work you're doing, it can help you stay motivated during difficult times, such as when you encounter challenges or setbacks.

  Choosing a niche that aligns with your interests can also make it easier to build a personal brand and establish yourself as an authority in your field. When you are passionate about a topic, you are more likely to have unique insights or perspectives that can set you apart from your competitors. This can help you attract a loyal following of customers who appreciate your expertise and value your content or offerings.

- **Assess your expertise:**

Assessing your expertise is an essential step in choosing a profitable niche. Consider your skills, education, and professional background, and evaluate how they relate to the niche you are interested in. If you have experience or expertise in a particular industry or topic, it can give you a competitive advantage and allow you to offer unique insights and solutions to your audience. Your expertise can also help you create high-quality content or products that meet the needs of your target audience.

However, it's important to note that you don't necessarily need to be an expert in your chosen niche to build a successful online business. You can always acquire new skills and knowledge through research, training, and networking. So, if you're passionate about a particular niche, but don't have a lot of experience in it, don't let that discourage you. Instead, be willing to learn and grow, and use your passion and enthusiasm to drive your success.

- **Consider the demand for your niche:**

When considering a niche, it's important to ensure that there is sufficient demand for the products or services you plan to offer. This means that there must be enough people interested in your niche to make it a viable business. Conducting market research to determine the size and demographics of your potential audience can help you gauge whether your niche is in high demand. You can use various online tools to research the popularity of different search terms and keywords related to your niche. By analyzing this data, you can identify any seasonal fluctuations or trends that may affect the demand for your products or services.

In addition to researching online trends, it's also important to check bestseller lists to determine which products or services are currently in high demand within your chosen niche. Analyzing the bestseller lists on Amazon or other online marketplaces can give you insights into the types of products or services that customers are interested in and the price range they are willing to pay for them. This information can help you tailor your offerings to meet customer needs and preferences and improve your chances of building a profitable online business. Ultimately, choosing a niche with sufficient demand is a critical step in building a sustainable and profitable online business.

- **Evaluate competition:**

Evaluating the competition in your potential niche is crucial to identifying opportunities for differentiation and innovation. Analyze your competitor's websites, social media profiles, and marketing strategies to understand what they're doing well and where they're falling short. Look for gaps in the market that you can fill with your unique perspective or expertise. For example, you might notice that your competitors are not providing enough educational content on a particular topic or are not catering to a specific demographic within the niche. By identifying these gaps, you can tailor your content, products, or services to meet the unfulfilled needs of your potential customers.

Furthermore, by analyzing your competitors' marketing strategies, you can gain valuable insights into what works and what doesn't in your niche. This information can help you refine your marketing strategy and identify potential collaborators or influencers who can help you expand your reach. However, it's important to remember that competition in your niche can also be an indicator of demand, so a healthy level of competition can be a good thing. The key is to differentiate yourself by providing unique value and building a strong personal brand that resonates with your target audience.

- **Look for opportunities to innovate:**

When selecting a niche for your online business, it's important to think about how you can differentiate yourself and innovate within your chosen industry. Consider what unique perspective or value you can bring to your audience that your competitors aren't offering. This could be through the use of emerging technologies, like virtual reality or artificial intelligence, or by approaching a traditional topic from a new angle.

By finding ways to innovate and differentiate yourself, you can attract a wider audience and establish yourself as a thought leader in your niche. This can ultimately lead to increased brand recognition and customer loyalty. It's important to continually monitor industry trends and developments and to be open to new ideas and strategies to stay ahead of the curve and maintain your competitive advantage.

Selecting a niche that aligns with your interests and expertise is critical to building a successful online business. By choosing a niche that you are passionate about and have some expertise in, you can create content that resonates with your audience and establish credibility and authority in your industry. Ensure that there is sufficient demand for your niche, evaluate your competition, and look for opportunities to innovate to stand out and provide unique value.

In summary, choosing the right niche is crucial to building a successful online business. By identifying your passion and talents, researching profitable niches, and selecting a niche that aligns with your interests and expertise, you can build a strong foundation for your online business. Remember that the key to success is to provide value to your audience, so choose a niche that you can be passionate about and that you can use to help others.

Chapter 2: Build Your Brand

Building a strong brand is essential for any successful online business. Your brand is what sets you apart from the competition and creates a connection with your audience. In this chapter, we will discuss how to build your brand by creating a memorable brand name and logo, establishing a strong online presence, building a website and social media presence, and creating a professional image.

1. Creating a memorable brand name and logo:

Creating a memorable brand name and logo is an essential part of building a successful online business. A strong brand name and logo can help you stand out from the competition and make a lasting impression on your audience.

Here are some tips for creating a memorable brand name and logo:

- **Reflect on the nature of your business:**

  When choosing a brand name, it's important to select one that accurately reflects the nature of your business, communicates what products or services you offer and is easy to understand and remember. Consider incorporating words related to your industry or niche and avoid complex or confusing terms. Also, choose a name that aligns with the tone you want to convey, whether it be playful, serious, or professional. Your brand name should ultimately reflect the essence of your business and make it easy for your audience to understand and remember what you offer.

- **Be unique:**

  Being unique is important when it comes to creating a brand name and logo. Your brand should be easily recognizable and memorable, and it should differentiate you from your competitors. Avoid generic names or logos that are similar to others in your industry, as this can lead to confusion and make it difficult for customers to distinguish your business from others. Consider using a creative or unconventional approach to create a brand name or logo that stands out and accurately represents your business. This can help you build a strong and memorable brand that resonates with your audience.

- **Be easily recognizable:**

Being easily recognizable is crucial for creating a strong brand. To achieve this, businesses need to develop a simple yet distinctive brand name and logo that reflects their values and messaging. Using unique colors, fonts, and imagery can help businesses stand out and make it easier for their audience to identify and remember their brand. Consistently using the brand name and logo across all marketing channels is also important in building brand recognition and reinforcing brand identity in the minds of the audience. By being easily recognizable, businesses can set themselves apart from the competition and build a strong brand image that resonates with their target audience.

- **Keep it simple:**

  Keeping your brand name and logo simple is important because it helps make them more memorable and recognizable. A complicated or convoluted name or logo can confuse your audience and make it harder for them to remember your brand. A straightforward name and logo also make it easier to communicate your brand to others and help establish a clear and consistent brand identity. When brainstorming your brand name and logo, try to focus on simplicity and clarity to create a memorable and effective brand.

- **Use appropriate colors and fonts:**

  Choosing appropriate colors and fonts for your brand name and logo is crucial in creating a strong and cohesive brand image that resonates with your audience. Colors have psychological effects on people and can convey different emotions and messages, so it's important to choose colors that are appropriate for your industry and the personality of your business. Fonts also play an important role in creating a brand image, and it's important to choose a font that reflects the personality of your brand and is legible and easy to read. When choosing colors and fonts, it's important to consider how they will look across different platforms and mediums, including your website, social media profiles, and marketing materials. Consistency in branding is key to building brand recognition and trust with your audience.

Once you have created a strong brand name and logo, it's essential to use them consistently across all your online and offline communications. This will help you establish a strong identity, build trust with your audience, and make your business more memorable.

2. Establishing a strong online presence:

Establishing a strong online presence is crucial for the success of your online business.
Here are some key steps to help you establish a strong online presence:

- **Create profiles on social media platforms:**

  Creating a strong social media presence is essential for building your brand and reaching your target audience. It starts with identifying the platforms your audience is most active on and creating complete profiles with your brand name and logo. Sharing valuable content that your audience will find interesting and engaging, and engaging with them by responding to comments, asking for feedback, and encouraging them to share your content, is critical for building a community around your brand. It's also important to promote your products or services without being too sales oriented, showcase them, and share customer reviews or testimonials. By building a loyal following and creating a strong social media presence, you can increase brand recognition, reach more people, and ultimately drive sales and growth for your business.

- **Set up a website:**

  Setting up a website is essential for building a strong online presence and establishing your brand. It's important to optimize your website for search engines, and ensure that it's mobile-friendly and easy to navigate. Design your website with your brand identity in mind, using consistent colors, fonts, and imagery to create a professional and cohesive look. Your website should communicate your business's value proposition clearly and concisely. Ensure that your website is user-friendly and optimized for search engines with relevant keywords and meta tags. Providing contact information and clear calls-to-action on your website is also crucial for customers to get in touch with you or make a purchase. By creating a well-designed, optimized, and user-friendly website, you can establish your brand online, build trust with your audience, and attract more customers to your business.

- **Optimize your online presence for search engines:**

Optimizing your online presence for search engines is a crucial step in increasing your visibility and driving traffic to your website. This involves using various techniques to help your website rank higher in search engine results pages, such as conducting keyword research to identify relevant and high-traffic keywords, creating well-organized and engaging website content that incorporates these keywords, building high-quality backlinks from reputable websites in your industry, and ensuring that your website is mobile-friendly, loads quickly, and has a clear and easy-to-navigate structure. By optimizing your online presence for search engines, you can improve your website's visibility, attract more traffic, and ultimately increase the success of your online business.

- **Consistent branding:**

Consistent branding is crucial for building a strong online presence and establishing brand recognition. When your brand name, logo, and messaging are consistent across all platforms, it creates a cohesive and memorable image for your business. This consistency not only helps to establish a strong brand identity but also builds trust and credibility with your audience.

To achieve this, use the same brand name and logo on all your online platforms and ensure that your messaging is consistent across all channels. By maintaining a consistent brand image, you can strengthen your brand recognition and build a loyal following of customers and supporters.

- **Engage with your audience:**

Engaging with your audience is essential for building a strong and loyal following for your brand. By responding to comments and messages promptly and sharing valuable content, you can establish yourself as an authority in your industry and show your audience that you value their feedback. Hosting Q&A sessions, running contests or giveaways, and conducting polls or surveys are also effective ways to engage with your audience and gather feedback. By actively engaging with your audience, you can build trust, increase brand loyalty, and encourage repeat business.

By establishing a strong online presence, you can build trust with your audience, increase your reach, and ultimately, drive more traffic and sales to your online business.

3. Building a website and social media presence:

Building a website and social media presence are essential components of establishing a strong online presence.
Here are some key considerations when building your website and social media presence:

- **Building a website:**

  Building a website involves several crucial considerations to ensure it represents your brand effectively and meets your audience's needs. Your website design should be visually appealing, professional, and consistent with your brand identity, using colors, fonts, and images that reflect your brand personality and messaging. You must also prioritize user-friendliness and easy navigation, optimizing your website for mobile devices, and search engines. Building a website can be done through a professional web designer or web development agency to tailor a custom website or through website builders like Wix, Squarespace, or WordPress.

- **Optimizing your website for search engines:**

Optimizing your website for search engines involves several key strategies that can improve your website's visibility in search engine results pages (SERPs). This includes using relevant keywords in your website content, but avoiding keyword stuffing, as well as ensuring that your website has high-quality, valuable content that is organized in a logical and user-friendly way. Additionally, building high-quality backlinks from other reputable websites to your website signals to search engines that your content is valuable and relevant. By focusing on these areas, you can improve your SEO and attract more potential customers to your website.

- **Establishing a social media presence:**

  Establishing a social media presence is essential for businesses to build an online community and connect with their target audience. To start, it's important to identify the social media platforms where your audience is most active and create consistent profiles with your brand name and logo. Sharing valuable content that's relevant to your niche and consistent with your brand messaging is crucial in building a successful social media presence. Platforms also provide the opportunity to promote your products or services, run targeted ads, and engage with your audience through comments, messages, and online conversations. By being responsive and encouraging feedback from your followers, you can build trust, establish a loyal following, and reach a wider audience.

- **Creating valuable content:**

  Creating valuable content is a fundamental aspect of building a successful online presence. It involves producing high-quality material that resonates with your target audience and provides value to them. To achieve this, it's crucial to understand your audience's interests and pain points and develop content ideas that cater to their needs while aligning with your brand messaging. The content you create should be relevant to your niche, offer value to your audience, and focus on quality over quantity. Consistency is also important, so it's essential to create a content calendar and stick to a consistent schedule for publishing your content. Overall, creating valuable content is an ongoing process that requires research, planning, and execution, but it can help you establish a strong online presence, build trust with your audience, and drive traffic to your website or social media profiles.

- **Engaging with your audience:**

Engaging with your audience is a crucial component of building a successful online presence. By responding to comments and messages promptly, participating in online conversations related to your niche, and encouraging feedback from your followers, you can establish a connection with your audience and build a sense of community around your brand. This not only helps you build trust with your audience but also enables you to understand their needs and preferences better, which can help you achieve your online goals such as building brand awareness, driving traffic to your website, or increasing sales.

4. Creating a professional image:

Creating a professional image is crucial to building trust with your audience and establishing credibility in your industry. Here are some key steps to creating a professional image for your brand:

- **Use high-quality images and videos:**

  To establish a strong online presence, it is crucial to use high-quality images and videos that showcase your brand's products, services, and story in a visually appealing way. Investing in professional photography and videography is necessary to avoid low-quality visuals that can make your brand look unprofessional. The visuals used should be relevant to your brand and audience, conveying the right emotions and values. By using high-quality visuals that stand out from the competition, your brand can create a lasting impression and grab the attention of your audience in today's visually-driven world.

- **Create engaging content:**

Creating engaging content is crucial to capturing and retaining your audience's attention and encouraging them to take action. To achieve this, it's important to know your target audience and their interests and create content that resonates with them. Well-written, informative, and easy-to-understand content that's free of spelling and grammar errors is essential. Including visuals like images, videos, and infographics can also make your content more visually appealing and memorable. Lastly, including a call to action at the end of your post can encourage your audience to engage with your content, follow your social media accounts, or visit your website, ultimately helping you establish a loyal following and a strong online presence.

- **Professionally present yourself:**

  Professionally presenting yourself is crucial to building a strong online presence. This includes not only your appearance but also your communication style and overall behavior. When presenting yourself online, it's important to maintain a positive and professional image. This can include using proper grammar and spelling in all communications, responding to messages and comments promptly and respectfully, and avoiding controversial or sensitive topics that could be considered offensive. It's also important to dress appropriately in any photos or videos you share online, as this can have an impact on how your brand is perceived. By professionally presenting yourself, you can build trust with your audience and establish yourself as a credible and respected authority in your niche.

- **Establish clear brand guidelines:**

  Establishing clear brand guidelines is crucial for building a strong and recognizable brand.

This involves defining your brand's visual identity, including color schemes, typography, and imagery, as well as defining your brand's tone of voice. Your visual identity and tone of voice should be consistent across all communications, including your website, social media profiles, and marketing materials. By doing so, you ensure consistency and establish a brand that is recognizable and memorable, which helps to build trust and loyalty with your audience and sets you apart from your competitors.

- **Have a professional website:**

A professional website is crucial to establishing a strong online presence for your brand, as it's often the first point of contact with potential customers or clients. To create a professional website, use professional web design and development tools to create a website that not only looks great but functions effectively as well. Optimize your website for all devices and search engines by using relevant keywords, meta tags, and descriptions in your website content, ensuring that your website loads quickly and has clean, optimized code. Include essential information such as your company's history, mission statement, contact information, and product or service offerings, as well as customer testimonials or reviews to establish trust and credibility with potential customers.

By taking these steps, you can create a professional image that helps build trust with your audience and sets you apart from competitors in your industry.

In summary, building a strong brand is essential for any successful online business. By creating a memorable brand name and logo, establishing a strong online presence, building a website and social media presence, and creating a professional image, you can establish a strong identity, build trust with your audience, and make your business more memorable.

Chapter 3: Create Valuable Content

In today's online landscape, creating valuable content is essential for attracting and retaining an audience. By providing content that is useful, informative, and engaging, you can establish credibility, build trust with your audience, and ultimately drive sales. Here are some key elements to keep in mind when creating valuable content:

1. Understanding the needs of your target audience:

Understanding the needs of your target audience is crucial for creating content that resonates with them and provides real value. To better understand your target audience, you can:

- **Conduct market research:**

  Market research is a crucial process for businesses to better understand their target audience. This involves collecting data on various aspects of the audience, such as demographics, interests, and behaviors. The information can be gathered through surveys, focus groups, and other research methods. By analyzing this data, businesses can gain valuable insights into their audience's needs and preferences. This can help in creating content that resonates with the audience and provide them with real value. It can also help in tailoring marketing efforts to specific segments of the audience and making informed business decisions. Overall, market research is an essential tool for businesses to stay relevant and competitive in their respective industries.

- **Use social media analytics:**

Social media analytics provide valuable data and insights into the behaviors and interests of your target audience. By analyzing metrics such as engagement rates, reach, and impressions, you can gain a deeper understanding of what type of content your audience likes and engages with the most. You can also use social media listening tools to monitor conversations related to your brand, industry, or niche. This information can help you identify trends, pain points, and topics of interest to your audience, allowing you to create content that resonates with them and provides value. Overall, using social media analytics is a powerful way to optimize your content strategy and improve engagement with your audience.

- **Identify pain points:**

  Identifying the pain points of your target audience is a crucial aspect of creating content that resonates with them. Pain points refer to the specific problems or challenges that your audience faces with your niche or industry. By identifying these pain points, you can create content that provides solutions and helps your audience overcome these challenges. This requires a deep understanding of your audience and their needs, as well as research into the specific pain points they experience. By addressing these pain points in your content, you can establish yourself as a trusted authority in your niche and build a loyal following.

- **Analyze competitors:**

  Analyzing your competitors' content and engagement is a great way to gain insights into what resonates with your target audience. By examining the type of content that performs well on their website and social media channels, you can identify patterns and trends in your niche. This information can help you create content that stands out from your competitors by providing unique value to your audience. Additionally, analyzing the engagement and interactions your competitors have with their audience can provide insights into what your target audience is looking for in terms of customer service and communication. By staying up-to-date with your competitors, you can ensure that you are creating content that meets the needs of your audience and differentiates you from the competition.

By understanding the needs of your target audience, you can create content that solves their problems and establishes you as a trusted authority in your niche.

2. Creating high-quality content that solves their problems:

Once you have a clear understanding of your audience's needs, you can start creating high-quality content that solves their problems. To create high-quality content that resonates with your audience, follow these tips:

- **Conduct thorough research:**

  Conducting thorough research is essential to creating content that resonates with your target audience. By researching the topics that are relevant to your niche, you can gain a better understanding of what your audience wants and needs. One effective way to research your audience is by using keyword research tools to identify the search terms they use when looking for information on your topic. You can also browse online forums and social media groups to see what questions people are asking and what problems they are trying to solve. This information can help you create content that provides value to your audience and addresses their specific needs and pain points. Additionally, thorough research can help you stay up to date with industry trends and best practices, ensuring that your content is relevant and informative.

- **Provide value:**

  Providing value to your audience is essential in building trust and credibility. Your content should aim to solve your audience's problems, answer their questions, and provide them with useful information that they can apply in their lives or work. Make sure your content is well-researched, accurate, and up-to-date. Use credible sources and provide references where appropriate. Additionally, aim to make your content actionable. Provide clear steps or tips that your audience can use to achieve their goals or solve their problems. By providing real value to your audience, you can establish yourself as a trusted authority in your niche and build a loyal following.

- **Use a variety of content formats:**

  Using a variety of content formats can help you reach a wider audience and keep them engaged with your brand. Some people prefer written content, while others prefer video or audio formats. By creating a mix of different formats, you can cater to all preferences and make your content more accessible to different types of learners. For example, visual learners may prefer infographics or videos, while auditory learners may prefer podcasts or audio guides. Additionally, using different formats can also help you repurpose your content and reach your audience on different platforms. For instance, you can turn a blog post into a video, an infographic, or a podcast, and promote it on different social media channels or other platforms to reach more people.

- **Optimize for SEO:**

To optimize your content for SEO, you should conduct keyword research to identify the keywords and phrases that your target audience is using to search for content related to your niche. Use these keywords strategically in your content, including in the title, meta description, headers, and throughout the body of your content. However, it's essential to use keywords naturally and avoid keyword stuffing, which can negatively impact your rankings. You should also ensure that your website has a clear structure and is mobile-friendly, as these factors also affect your search engine rankings. Additionally, building backlinks to your content from other reputable websites can also help improve your SEO.

- **Be consistent:**

Consistency is a crucial element of content creation. Establishing a content calendar and sticking to it ensures that your audience knows when to expect new content from you. This builds trust and reliability, which are essential for building a loyal following. Creating a consistent posting schedule also helps you stay organized and focused on your content creation goals. Consistency also applies to the quality of your content. Ensure that each piece of content is of high quality, valuable, and aligns with your brand's voice and messaging. Consistency in both posting schedule and content quality helps establish you as an authority in your niche and keeps your audience engaged and coming back for more.

By creating high-quality content that solves your audience's problems, you can establish a loyal following and build a strong reputation in your niche.

3. Developing a content strategy:

To consistently create valuable content, it's important to develop a content strategy. This includes setting goals, defining your target audience, creating a content calendar, and deciding on the types of content you will create. A content strategy is a plan that outlines the key elements of your content creation process. It includes the following:

- **Setting goals:**

  Setting clear goals is an essential part of creating a successful content strategy. It helps to define the purpose of your content and the specific outcomes you want to achieve. For instance, if your goal is to increase website traffic, you might focus on creating SEO-optimized blog posts that attract more organic traffic. Alternatively, if your goal is to generate leads, you might create gated content like eBooks or whitepapers that require users to fill out a form to access. Defining your goals helps you to create content that is aligned with your business objectives, measure your progress and success, and make adjustments as needed. Additionally, it provides direction and focuses for your content creation efforts and helps you prioritize your time and resources effectively.

- **Defining your target audience:**

Defining your target audience is a critical step in developing a successful content strategy. To effectively create content that resonates with your audience, you need to understand their demographics, interests, challenges, and preferences. Demographics include factors such as age, gender, location, and education level. Interests may include hobbies, values, and lifestyles. Challenges may refer to the pain points and problems they face related to your niche, and preferences may include their preferred content formats and platforms.

By understanding your target audience, you can create content that speaks directly to their needs, interests, and pain points. This will help you establish a connection with them and build trust, ultimately leading to increased engagement and conversions. You can gather information about your target audience through market research, social media analytics, and other tools. This information can then be used to tailor your content to their specific needs and preferences.

- **Creating a content calendar:**

Creating a content calendar is an essential component of a successful content strategy. By planning your content, you can stay organized and ensure that you are consistently delivering valuable content to your audience. A content calendar allows you to map out your content publishing schedule, including the dates, channels, and types of content you will create.

This helps you avoid last-minute content creation and ensures that you are prepared with high-quality content that resonates with your target audience. It also helps you balance your content mix and avoid content gaps or overlaps. By being consistent and organized with your content publishing, you can build a loyal following and establish yourself as a trusted authority in your niche.

- **Deciding on the types of content:**

When deciding on the types of content to create for your audience, it's essential to consider your niche and your target audience's preferences. Different types of content cater to different learning styles and consumption habits. Blog posts are a popular and versatile format that allows for long-form, in-depth content. Videos and podcasts are great for those who prefer audiovisual content and can be a more engaging way to communicate with your audience. Infographics are ideal for presenting complex data and statistics in a visually appealing way. Social media posts are perfect for reaching a broader audience and engaging with your followers more casually and conversationally. By identifying the types of content that work best for your niche and audience, you can create a diverse range of content that caters to different preferences and maximizes your reach.

By developing a content strategy, you can streamline your content creation process, create content that resonates with your audience, and achieve your business goals.

4. Creating various types of content:

Creating various types of content can help you keep your audience engaged and interested in your brand.
Here are some key points to keep in mind when creating different types of content:

- **Blog posts:**

  Blogging is an essential content type for any content strategy, as it allows businesses to provide detailed information on specific topics related to their niche. Blog posts should be well-written, informative, and offer actionable advice or solutions to your audience's challenges. They can help establish a brand's credibility and authority in their industry, increase website traffic, and generate leads. To create effective blog posts, it's important to conduct thorough research, write clearly and concisely, and use visuals to enhance the content. Additionally, including a call to action can encourage readers to engage with the brand and potentially convert into customers.

- **Videos:**

Videos are a powerful content type that can help you engage your audience on a deeper level. They can be used to showcase your products or services, demonstrate how to use them, or offer insights into your business. Whether it's a product demo, a how-to tutorial, or an interview with industry experts, videos should be high-quality and visually appealing to capture your audience's attention. To make sure your videos offer value, they should provide actionable insights or solutions to your audience's challenges. Consider experimenting with different video formats, such as explainer videos, behind-the-scenes glimpses, or customer testimonials, to see what resonates best with your audience.

- **Podcasts:**

  Podcasts have been growing in popularity in recent years and offer a unique way to connect with your audience. They can be used to share your knowledge and expertise, interview industry experts or influencers, or engage in conversations with your audience. When creating podcasts, it's important to have a clear idea of what topics you want to cover and who your target audience is. Your podcast should be well-produced and have a clear format and structure that your listeners can easily follow. You should also aim to create engaging and interesting content that offers value to your listeners, whether it's through sharing insights, offering advice, or providing entertainment. Additionally, promoting your podcast on various platforms and engaging with your listeners can help grow your audience and build a loyal following.

- **Infographics:**

  Infographics are a visually compelling way to communicate complex information to your audience. They are particularly useful when you need to present data, statistics, or other information that may be difficult to understand in written form. The key to a successful infographic is to design it in a way that is easy to comprehend, visually appealing, and shareable. A well-designed infographic should have a clear hierarchy of information, use appropriate colors and fonts, and include relevant visuals such as charts, graphs, or icons. Infographics can be shared on social media platforms or embedded on your website or blog, making them an effective way to increase your brand's visibility and engagement.

By creating a variety of content types, you can keep your audience engaged and provide value in different ways. It's important to experiment with different formats and see what resonates best with your audience.

Chapter 4: Build an Email List

In today's digital age, email marketing has become one of the most effective ways to reach and engage with your target audience. Building an email list enables you to establish direct communication with your subscribers, providing you with a unique opportunity to build a relationship with them and promote your products or services. By offering a lead magnet that provides value to your subscribers, you can entice them to sign up for your email list, permitting you to contact them directly with relevant and useful information. From there, you can use email marketing to regularly provide your subscribers with valuable content, build trust, and establish yourself as an authority in your niche. An email list can also be a valuable source of revenue for your business, allowing you to monetize your list through affiliate marketing and product launches. Overall, building an email list is a crucial component of any successful online business strategy, enabling you to build strong relationships with your audience, establish trust, and ultimately drive more sales and revenue for your business.

Here are some key steps to building an email list:

1. Creating a lead magnet to entice subscribers:

A lead magnet is a powerful marketing tool that can help grow your email list and ultimately, your business. The aim is to capture the attention of potential subscribers and persuade them to join your email list. It's an incentive that you offer to your audience in exchange for their contact information, usually an email address. By offering a lead magnet, you provide your audience with an opportunity to learn more about your brand or industry while also building a relationship with them.

When creating a lead magnet, it's essential to offer something of value that is relevant to your niche or industry. This could be in the form of an e-book, a whitepaper, a checklist, a free trial, or any other valuable resource. The key is to make sure that the lead magnet is high quality and offers a quick win or solution to a specific problem that your audience is facing. This helps to build trust and credibility with your audience, which can lead to more subscribers and ultimately, more business.

An effective lead magnet can make a significant difference in your email list growth. It can increase the number of subscribers and improve the overall quality of your list. With more subscribers, you can build a community around your brand or product and use email marketing to engage with them regularly. This is important for building long-term relationships with your audience and ultimately, increasing sales and revenue.

To create a compelling lead magnet, you need to understand your target audience and their needs. You should research to identify their pain points, interests, and preferences. This information can help you create a lead magnet that resonates with your audience and offers value. By providing a lead magnet that addresses a specific pain point or offers a solution, you can increase the chances of your audience signing up for your email list.

In summary, a lead magnet is a valuable marketing tool that can help grow your email list and ultimately, your business. By offering something of value that is relevant to your audience, you can capture their attention and build a relationship with them. Creating an effective lead magnet requires understanding your target audience and their needs, and providing a high-quality resource that offers a quick win or solution to a specific problem. With a compelling lead magnet, you can significantly increase the number of email subscribers and build a valuable email list that you can use for marketing and sales purposes.

2. Using email marketing to build relationships with subscribers:

Email marketing is a powerful way to connect with your subscribers and build long-term relationships with them. After all, the people on your email list have already shown an interest in your business by signing up, so it's important to keep them engaged and informed. One of the most important aspects of email marketing is providing value to your subscribers. This means sending regular emails that are informative, interesting, and helpful. By doing so, you can establish yourself as an authority in your niche and gain the trust and loyalty of your subscribers.

To create effective email marketing campaigns, you need to segment your list according to your subscribers' interests and preferences. By doing so, you can send targeted messages that are more likely to resonate with your audience. For example, you could create separate segments for subscribers who have purchased a specific product, or who have shown interest in a particular topic on your website. By sending relevant messages to each segment, you can increase the likelihood that your subscribers will open and engage with your emails.

Another important aspect of email marketing is choosing the right frequency for your messages. You want to stay top-of-mind with your subscribers, but you also don't want to overwhelm them with too many emails. Generally, it's best to send one to two emails per week, but the frequency will depend on your audience and the type of content you are sending. It's important to track your email open rates and click-through rates to see how your subscribers are responding to your messages and adjust your strategy accordingly.

When crafting your email messages, it's important to focus on providing value to your subscribers. This means avoiding overly promotional language and instead, offering helpful tips, insights, or resources that your audience will find valuable. You can also use your email campaigns to promote your blog posts, videos, or other content that you've published on your website. This can help drive traffic to your site and increase engagement with your brand.

Finally, it's important to use a strong call-to-action (CTA) in your email messages. Your CTA should encourage your subscribers to take a specific action, such as visiting your website, signing up for a free trial, or making a purchase. It's important to make your CTA clear and easy to follow and to use a sense of urgency to encourage immediate action. By using a strong CTA, you can increase the effectiveness of your email marketing campaigns and drive more conversions.

Overall, email marketing is a powerful way to build relationships with your subscribers and promote your brand. By providing value, targeting your messages, and using strong CTAs, you can create effective email campaigns that drive engagement and conversions. It's important to track your metrics and adjust your strategy as needed to ensure that your email marketing efforts are successful over the long term.

3. Monetizing your email list through affiliate marketing and product launches:

Monetizing your email list is an important step in growing your business, and there are multiple strategies you can use to do so. One popular approach is affiliate marketing, which involves promoting other people's products or services to your email list and earning a commission for any resulting sales. This can be a win-win situation for both you and the product owner, as you get a percentage of the sale and they get exposure to a new audience.

To successfully monetize your email list through affiliate marketing, it's important to carefully choose products or services that align with your audience's interests and needs. You don't want to promote something just for the sake of earning a commission, as this can damage the trust you've built with your subscribers. Instead, focus on promoting high-quality products that you believe will genuinely benefit your audience.

Another way to monetize your email list is through product launches. This involves creating and launching your products to your email list and generating revenue from sales. This approach can be particularly lucrative if you have a large and engaged email list, as your subscribers are already familiar with your brand and more likely to buy from you.

When creating your products, it's important to choose something that is aligned with your audience's needs and interests. This could be a course, ebook, or other digital product that provides value and helps your audience solve a problem. You'll also need to create a compelling launch strategy to get your subscribers excited about the new product and motivate them to make a purchase.

In addition to affiliate marketing and product launches, there are other ways to monetize your email list. For example, you could offer sponsored content or advertising opportunities to businesses that want to reach your audience. You could also offer premium content or services to your email subscribers for a fee.

Ultimately, the key to successfully monetizing your email list is to provide consistent value to your subscribers and build trust over time. If your audience feels like they can rely on you for high-quality recommendations and resources, they will be more likely to purchase products or services that you promote or create. However, if you prioritize making money over providing value, you may end up alienating your audience and damaging your brand reputation. So, always keep your subscribers' needs and interests top of mind when considering how to monetize your email list.

Chapter 5: Affiliate Marketing

Affiliate marketing is an effective way to earn money through your online business by promoting other people's products and receiving a commission on each sale made through your unique affiliate link. By choosing affiliate products that are relevant to your niche and offer a good commission rate, you can increase your chances of profitability. Building trust with your audience is crucial before promoting any affiliate products and can be achieved by consistently providing valuable content, being transparent about your affiliate relationships, and promoting only products that you genuinely believe in and have used yourself. Creating effective content that highlights the benefits of the product and how it can solve your audience's problems is key to successfully promoting affiliate products, and including your unique affiliate link in your content makes it easy for your audience to make a purchase. You can maximize your earnings through affiliate marketing by promoting products that offer a higher commission rate or have a high-ticket price, leveraging email marketing to promote affiliate products to your subscribers, negotiating higher commission rates with affiliate programs, and joining affiliate networks to access a wider range of products to promote.

To succeed in affiliate marketing, there are several key strategies to keep in mind:

1. Finding profitable affiliate products:

Finding profitable affiliate products is crucial to your success in affiliate marketing. The first step in finding these products is to identify your niche and target audience. Once you have a clear understanding of your niche, you can start researching products that are relevant to your audience's needs and interests.

When choosing affiliate products, it's important to consider the commission rate. Look for products that offer a good commission rate so that you can earn a substantial income from promoting them. However, be careful not to choose products based solely on the commission rate. You want to promote products that align with your values and provide value to your audience.

Another factor to consider when choosing affiliate products is the conversion rate. Look for products that have a high conversion rate as this means that they are more likely to generate sales. You can research the conversion rate by checking the product's sales page, analyzing the product's history of sales, and reading customer reviews. A high conversion rate is a good indication that the product is in demand and that your audience is more likely to make a purchase.

It's also important to promote quality products that your audience will find valuable. Look for products that have positive customer reviews and feedback. You want to promote products that will help your audience solve their problems and meet their needs. Promoting low-quality products that don't deliver on their promises will damage your reputation and credibility with your audience.

When researching affiliate products, it's also a good idea to look at the competition. Check to see if other affiliates are promoting the same product and how they are promoting it. This will give you an idea of how you can differentiate yourself and stand out from the competition. Consider creating unique content and highlighting different aspects of the product to make it more appealing to your audience.

Overall, finding profitable affiliate products requires research, consideration of the commission rate and conversion rate, promotion of quality products, and differentiation from the competition. By choosing the right affiliate products to promote, you can earn a substantial income and provide value to your audience.

2. Building trust with your audience:

Building trust with your audience is crucial in affiliate marketing. When you promote affiliate products, you are essentially recommending them to your audience, and they trust your judgment. Therefore, it's important to build a strong relationship with your audience based on trust and credibility.

One way to build trust with your audience is by consistently providing valuable content that meets their needs and helps them solve their problems. This content can be in the form of blog posts, videos, podcasts, or any other type of content that is relevant to your niche. By consistently providing value, your audience will see you as a helpful resource and will be more likely to trust your recommendations.

Another important aspect of building trust is being transparent about your affiliate relationships. This means disclosing that you are an affiliate and may earn a commission if someone purchases through your link. Being transparent shows that you are honest and trustworthy, and it also helps to comply with legal requirements for disclosing affiliate relationships.

In addition to providing valuable content and being transparent, it's important to only promote products that you genuinely believe in and have used yourself. If you promote products that you don't believe in or have no experience with, your audience will quickly lose trust in you. On the other hand, if you promote products that you have used and can vouch for, your audience will see that you have their best interests in mind and will be more likely to trust your recommendations.

One way to ensure that you only promote quality products is by doing research and choosing products that have a high conversion rate and positive customer reviews. This shows that the product is in demand and that people are satisfied with their purchase. It also helps to choose products that are relevant to your niche and will be of value to your audience.

Overall, building trust with your audience is crucial in affiliate marketing. By consistently providing valuable content, being transparent about your affiliate relationships, and only promoting products that you genuinely believe in and have used yourself, you can build a strong relationship with your audience based on trust and credibility. This will ultimately lead to more sales and higher earnings from your affiliate marketing efforts.

3. Promoting affiliate products effectively:

Promoting affiliate products effectively is crucial to the success of your affiliate marketing efforts. The first step is to create high-quality content that showcases the benefits of the product and how it can solve your audience's problems. This content can come in the form of blog posts, videos, social media posts, or even email newsletters. Whatever format you choose, make sure it's engaging and valuable to your audience.

When creating your content, it's important to keep in mind that you are not just selling a product, but rather a solution to your audience's needs. Focus on the benefits and outcomes of the product, rather than just its features. For example, instead of simply listing the technical specifications of a camera, you could create content that demonstrates how it can help your audience take stunning photos and capture memories they'll cherish forever.

Another key element of promoting affiliate products effectively is including your unique affiliate link in your content. This makes it easy for your audience to make a purchase and ensures that you receive credit for any sales made through your link. You can use trackable links to see which of your content pieces are driving the most sales, allowing you to optimize your efforts accordingly.

Social media can be a powerful tool for promoting affiliate products. You can use platforms like Instagram and YouTube to create visually appealing content that showcases the product and its benefits. Make sure to include your affiliate link in your posts and use relevant hashtags to reach a wider audience. You can also partner with influencers in your niche to promote the product to their followers, increasing your reach and credibility.

In addition to creating your content, you can also leverage existing content to promote affiliate products. For example, you could reach out to bloggers or YouTubers in your niche and offer to sponsor a post or video featuring your product. This can be a great way to reach a new audience and tap into their existing trust and engagement with the content creator.

Finally, it's important to always disclose your affiliate relationships to your audience. This builds trust and transparency with your audience and ensures that you are complying with legal guidelines. You can include a disclaimer in your content or on your website, stating that you may receive a commission for any purchases made through your affiliate links.

Overall, promoting affiliate products effectively requires a strategic approach that focuses on creating valuable content, including your affiliate link, and leveraging existing platforms and influencers. With the right tactics, you can build a successful affiliate marketing business and generate significant revenue.

4. Maximizing your earnings through affiliate marketing:

One way to maximize your earnings through affiliate marketing is to focus on promoting products that offer a higher commission rate. By promoting products with a higher commission rate, you can earn more money per sale and increase your overall revenue. When looking for affiliate products to promote, consider the commission rate as well as the product's relevance to your niche and audience.

Another way to maximize your earnings is by promoting products with a high-ticket price. While these products may have a lower conversion rate, they can lead to higher earnings per sale. This is because you will earn a percentage of the total sale price, which can be significant for higher-priced items. Keep in mind that high-ticket items require more convincing to sell, so you will need to create high-quality content that demonstrates the value of the product.

Email marketing is another effective way to maximize your earnings through affiliate marketing. By building an email list, you can promote affiliate products directly to your subscribers. This allows you to target people who have already shown an interest in your niche or the products you promote. To effectively promote affiliate products through email marketing, create engaging content that highlights the benefits of the product and includes your affiliate link.

Creating product reviews or comparisons can also help you maximize your earnings through affiliate marketing. By providing detailed information and an honest assessment of the product, you can help your audience make informed purchasing decisions. This can increase your conversions and ultimately lead to higher earnings. When creating product reviews or comparisons, be sure to disclose that you are an affiliate and include your affiliate link.

Negotiating higher commission rates with affiliate programs can also increase your earnings. If you have a strong following and can demonstrate that you can drive significant sales, some affiliate programs may be willing to offer a higher commission rate. This can lead to a significant increase in earnings over time.

Finally, joining affiliate networks can provide access to a wider range of products to promote. Affiliate networks connect advertisers with affiliates, providing a centralized platform for finding and promoting products. By joining an affiliate network, you can find new products to promote and expand your earning potential.

In summary, to maximize your earnings through affiliate marketing, focus on promoting products with a higher commission rate or high-ticket price, leverage email marketing, create product reviews or comparisons, negotiate higher commission rates with affiliate programs, and join affiliate networks to access a wider range of products to promote. Remember to always prioritize promoting products that align with your niche and audience to maintain trust and credibility with your audience.

Chapter 6: Sell Digital Products

Selling Digital products is one of the best ways to generate revenue.

1. Creating and selling digital products:

Creating and selling digital products can be an effective way to earn income from your online business. One of the main benefits of digital products is that they can be created once and sold multiple times, allowing for passive income generation. To create successful digital products, it's important to focus on providing value to your audience and solving their problems. This can be done by identifying common pain points or challenges within your niche and developing products that offer solutions.

When creating digital products, it's important to consider the format and delivery method. eBooks, for example, are often delivered as downloadable PDFs, while online courses may be delivered through a learning management system. Webinars can be conducted life or recorded and made available for on-demand viewing. Printables, such as planners or checklists, can be delivered as downloadable files or physical products.

Developing a sales funnel is crucial for effectively selling digital products. A sales funnel is a series of steps that guide a prospect toward purchasing your product. This can include a landing page that highlights the benefits of your product and encourages visitors to opt-in to your email list. An email sequence can then be used to provide additional value and build trust with your audience before presenting your product offer. The checkout process should be smooth and user-friendly, making it easy for customers to purchase your product.

Upsells and downsells can be used to maximize your earnings from selling digital products. Upsells are additional products or services that you offer after the initial purchase, while downsells are alternative or lower-priced offers if the prospect declines the upsell. This can increase your revenue per customer and provide additional value to your audience.

To grow your digital product business, it's important to continue creating new products that solve your audience's problems and meet their needs. You can also optimize your sales funnel to improve conversion rates and increase revenue per customer. Promoting your products through various marketing channels, such as social media, email marketing, and paid advertising, can also help you reach new audiences and grow your business.

Staying up-to-date with trends in your niche is also important for growing a successful digital product business. This can involve researching popular topics and keywords, analyzing your competition, and staying on top of industry news and developments. By consistently providing value to your audience and adapting to changes in your niche, you can continue to grow and thrive as a digital product creator and seller.

2. Developing a sales funnel:

A sales funnel is a crucial aspect of selling digital products because it helps to convert prospects into customers. The first step is to create a landing page that captures the attention of your audience and provides them with a compelling reason to take action. This can be achieved by offering a free download, a discount, or access to exclusive content.

Once a prospect has entered your sales funnel, the next step is to use email marketing to nurture them and build a relationship. This can involve sending a series of automated emails that provide value, such as helpful tips or free resources. The goal is to keep your audience engaged and interested in your product, so they are more likely to make a purchase.

As the prospect moves through your sales funnel, it's important to continue providing value and building trust. This can be done by creating content that addresses their pain points and offers solutions. For example, if you are selling an online course on how to start a business, you might create blog posts or videos that provide tips on finding a niche or developing a business plan.

When it comes to the checkout process, it's important to make it as smooth and user-friendly as possible. This means providing clear instructions, offering multiple payment options, and ensuring that your website is secure. You can also use upsells and downsells to increase your revenue per customer and offer additional value.

Another important aspect of developing a sales funnel is tracking your results and making adjustments as needed. This can involve using analytics to see which pages are converting the most prospects and which emails are getting the best response rates. By continually optimizing your sales funnel, you can improve your conversion rates and maximize your revenue.

Ultimately, the success of your sales funnel depends on the value you provide to your audience and the level of trust you can build. By focusing on creating high-quality digital products and providing a seamless customer experience, you can establish a strong reputation and build a loyal customer base.

In summary, developing a sales funnel is a key component of selling digital products. It involves creating a landing page, using email marketing to nurture prospects, providing value and building trust, optimizing the checkout process, and tracking your results. By following these steps and continuously improving your sales funnel, you can increase your conversion rates and generate more revenue from your digital products.

3. Using upsells and downsells:

Upselling and downselling are powerful techniques used to boost sales and revenue in digital product businesses. Upselling involves offering customers an additional product or service after they have made a purchase, while downselling is offering an alternative or lower-priced product when the customer has declined the initial upsell.

The idea behind upselling and downselling is to increase the customer's purchase value and provide them with more value for their money. This is particularly effective in digital product businesses because it costs little to no additional resources to offer an upsell or downsell to a customer.

To effectively use upsells and downsells in your digital product business, you should first analyze your customer's needs and preferences. By understanding your customer's needs, you can offer upsells and downsells that are relevant and useful to them. For example, if your customer has just purchased an online course on digital marketing, you can offer them an upsell for a one-on-one consultation with a digital marketing expert.

Another way to effectively use upsells and downsells is to ensure that the additional product or service offered provides significant value to the customer. If the upsell or downsell is not useful or relevant to the customer, they may not be interested in making the additional purchase.

In addition, you should make sure that the upsell or downsell is offered at the right time in the sales funnel. The upsell or downsell should not be offered too early, as the customer may not have built enough trust in your product or brand. On the other hand, offering the upsell or downsell too late in the sales funnel may cause the customer to lose interest.

Upselling and downselling can also be used as a way to retain customers and increase customer loyalty. By offering customers additional value and personalized attention, they are more likely to return for future purchases and recommend your products to others.

It's important to note that upselling and downselling should be used sparingly and thoughtfully. Bombarding customers with too many offers can be overwhelming and lead to a negative customer experience. Instead, focus on offering targeted and relevant upsells and downsells that add value to the customer's purchase.

Finally, it's important to track and analyze the effectiveness of your upsell and downsell offers. This can be done through analytics tools and customer feedback. By analyzing the data, you can identify which offers are most effective and make adjustments to improve your sales funnel.

In conclusion, using upsells and downsells can be an effective way to increase revenue and provide additional value to your customers in a digital product business. By understanding your customer's needs, offering relevant and useful offers, and tracking the effectiveness of your offers, you can optimize your sales funnel and improve customer satisfaction.

4. Growing your digital product business:

Once you have established your digital product business, it's essential to focus on growth to increase revenue and reach a wider audience. One way to do this is by creating new products that solve different problems for your audience or by expanding on existing products. By offering more options, you can appeal to a broader range of customers and generate more revenue.

Optimizing your sales funnel is another critical step to growing your digital product business. You can continually test and tweak your funnel to improve conversion rates and increase sales. You can analyze customer behavior and adjust your messaging, offers, and pricing to better suit their needs and interests. By making the purchase process smoother and more user-friendly, you can encourage more customers to buy and increase your revenue.

Promoting your products through various marketing channels is also crucial for growing your digital product business. You can leverage social media, email marketing, search engine optimization, and paid advertising to reach a wider audience and attract new customers. By creating compelling and valuable content that resonates with your audience and using targeted ads, you can drive more traffic to your sales funnel and increase sales.

Partnering with affiliates and influencers is another effective strategy for growing your digital product business. You can offer a commission to affiliates who promote your products to their audience, expanding your reach and generating more sales. Influencers can also help you reach a broader audience and increase brand awareness by sharing their experiences with your products.

Continuing to provide value to your audience is vital for the growth of your digital product business. By staying up-to-date with the latest trends in your niche and continually creating high-quality products that solve real problems, you can build a loyal following and attract new customers. You can also offer ongoing support and resources to your customers to help them get the most out of your products, strengthening your relationship and building trust.

It's important to track and measure your growth to understand what's working and what's not. By analyzing metrics such as conversion rates, traffic sources, and customer feedback, you can identify areas for improvement and adjust your strategy accordingly. By continually adapting and evolving, you can stay ahead of the competition and continue to grow your digital product business.

In summary, growing a digital product business requires ongoing effort and attention to detail. By creating new products, optimizing your sales funnel, promoting your products through various channels, partnering with affiliates and influencers, providing ongoing value to your audience, and tracking your growth, you can increase revenue, reach a wider audience, and build a successful digital product business.

Chapter 7: Start Dropshipping

Dropshipping is a unique business model that allows entrepreneurs to sell products without holding inventory. Unlike traditional e-commerce businesses, dropshippers work with suppliers who store and ship the products directly to their customers. This eliminates the need to invest in and manage inventory, which can significantly lower upfront costs and reduce risk. Dropshipping also offers a wider range of products to sell, as entrepreneurs can source products from suppliers all over the world.

However, dropshippers have less control over the quality of products and shipping times, which can impact the customer experience. Despite its limitations, dropshipping has become a popular way for entrepreneurs to start and grow online businesses.

Here are some key steps to start a dropshipping business:

1. Understand dropshipping:

To understand dropshipping, it is essential to know that it is a business model that has gained popularity in recent years. It allows individuals to start an e-commerce business without having to invest a significant amount of money in inventory. The main advantage of dropshipping is that you can sell products without holding inventory, which means you don't need to store or handle products.

In dropshipping, you work with a supplier who ships the products directly to your customers. This means that when a customer places an order on your website, you forward the order to the supplier who then ships the product to the customer. The supplier is responsible for inventory management, shipping, and handling of returns.

The main advantage of dropshipping is that it requires a minimal upfront investment. This is because you don't have to purchase inventory before making sales, and you don't have to pay for warehousing or storage space. Additionally, dropshipping allows you to offer a wider range of products than you could if you were holding inventory.

However, dropshipping also has some limitations that are important to consider. Since you are not in charge of shipping or handling the products, you have less control over the quality of the product and the speed of shipping. This means that if a customer has a negative experience, it reflects on your business, even if the issue was caused by the supplier.

Another limitation of dropshipping is that profit margins may be lower compared to businesses that hold inventory. This is because the supplier may charge a higher price for the product, which leaves less room for profit.

To overcome these limitations, it's important to choose a reliable supplier with a track record of timely and reliable shipping. This can be done by researching and checking reviews of suppliers before you start working with them. Additionally, you can create a system for quality control by testing products before adding them to your store and providing excellent customer service to handle any issues that arise.

In conclusion, dropshipping is a business model that has advantages and limitations. It is an attractive option for individuals who want to start an e-commerce business without investing significant amounts of money upfront. However, it's important to understand that dropshipping requires careful research and planning to ensure success. By choosing reliable suppliers, testing products, and providing excellent customer service, you can overcome the limitations of dropshipping and build a successful e-commerce business.

2. Identify profitable products to sell:

Identifying profitable products to sell is a crucial step in starting a successful dropshipping business. Researching your niche and finding products with high demand and profit margins can help ensure the success of your business.

One way to identify profitable products is by using tools like Google Trends and keyword research. Google Trends can give you insights into the popularity of certain products over time, while keyword research can help you understand the search volume for specific keywords related to your niche. By analyzing these tools, you can get an idea of what products are in high demand and what keywords people are searching for.

Another approach to identifying profitable products is by analyzing your competitors. Look at what products they are selling and how they are marketing them. Are there any gaps in the market that you can fill with unique products or better marketing strategies? By analyzing your competition, you can get a better understanding of what products are popular and how you can differentiate yourself from your competitors.

Additionally, it's important to consider the profit margins of the products you are considering selling. Low-priced products may have high demand, but the profit margin may be too low to sustain your business in the long term. Look for products that have high enough profit margins to cover your expenses and allow for growth.

When identifying profitable products, it's also important to consider the shipping costs and times associated with each product. Dropshipping relies on timely and reliable shipping, so it's crucial to work with suppliers who can provide fast and efficient shipping. Additionally, if a product has high shipping costs, it may not be profitable to sell, as customers may be deterred by the additional expense.

Finally, it's important to consider the seasonality of certain products. Some products may be popular during certain times of the year, such as a holiday or seasonal products. While these products can be profitable during their peak season, they may not be sustainable throughout the year. Consider diversifying your product offerings to include evergreen products that can be sold year-round.

Overall, identifying profitable products requires thorough research and analysis. By using tools like Google Trends, analyzing your competitors, considering profit margins and shipping costs, and accounting for seasonality, you can identify products with high demand and profit potential.

3. Find a reliable supplier:

Finding a reliable supplier is a crucial step in building a successful dropshipping business. You want to work with a supplier that provides high-quality products and delivers them to your customers in a timely and reliable manner. Here are some key tips for finding a reliable supplier:

- **Do your research:**
  Start by researching potential suppliers online. Look for reviews and testimonials from other dropshippers and check their reputation. You can also ask for recommendations in online forums and social media groups.

- **Contact potential suppliers:**
  Once you've identified a few potential suppliers, reach out to them to learn more about their products and services. Ask about their shipping times, pricing, and return policies. You should also ask for samples of their products to ensure their quality.

- **Check their inventory:**
  Make sure the supplier has the products you want to sell in stock and ready to ship. You don't want to sell a product only to find out that it's out of stock or has a long lead time.

- **Evaluate their communication:**
  A good supplier should be responsive and easy to communicate with. They should be able to answer your questions quickly and provide updates on your orders as needed.

- **Test their shipping:**
  Once you've chosen a supplier, place a few test orders to ensure their shipping times and packaging meet your standards. You can also have a friend or family member place an order to ensure the customer experience is smooth.

- **Build a relationship:**
  Once you've found a reliable supplier, work to build a strong relationship with them. This can include communicating regularly, offering feedback on their products and services, and working together to improve your business.

Overall, finding a reliable supplier is essential for building a successful dropshipping business. Take your time to research and evaluate potential suppliers to ensure you're working with a partner who can help you grow your business.

4. Build a dropshipping website:

To build a dropshipping website, you can create an e-commerce store using a platform that provides features for online stores like inventory management, payment gateways, and shipping options. Shopify and WooCommerce are popular platforms for building e-commerce stores, but there are other options available as well.

When creating your store, it's important to choose a design that's visually appealing and easy to navigate. You can choose from a variety of templates and customize them to suit your branding and product offerings. It's also important to ensure that your website is optimized for mobile devices, as more and more customers are shopping on their phones.

Once you have your store set up, you can start adding products to your inventory. With drop shipping, you don't need to hold any physical inventory, so you'll be importing product listings from your supplier. It's important to ensure that the product descriptions and images are high-quality and accurately represent the product.

To automate the process of fulfilling orders, you can use a dropshipping integration that syncs your store with your supplier's inventory and shipping information. This will allow orders to be automatically fulfilled and shipped to your customers without any manual intervention on your part. However, it's important to ensure that your supplier is reliable and has a good track record of fulfilling orders on time.

In addition to setting up your website, it's important to also set up your payment gateway so that customers can easily make purchases on your site. You'll need to choose a payment gateway that's secure and reliable, and that supports the types of payments that your customers are likely to use.

Finally, it's important to test your website thoroughly before launching it to the public. This will help you identify any issues or areas for improvement, such as slow page load times or confusing navigation. By taking the time to build a high-quality dropshipping website, you'll be able to provide a positive shopping experience for your customers and set your business up for success.

5. Optimize your website for conversions:

After building your dropshipping website, it's important to optimize it for conversions to maximize your sales. The first step is to ensure that your website is easy to navigate and user-friendly. This means having clear menus and categories, a search bar, and a well-organized product page.

Additionally, your website should have clear calls to action (CTAs) throughout. A CTA is a button or link that encourages visitors to take a specific action, such as "Add to Cart" or "Buy Now." These buttons should be prominent and easy to find on each product page, as well as on your website's main pages.

One key element of optimizing your website for conversions is having high-quality product images. Your product images should be clear, and well-lit, and showcase the product from multiple angles. This will give customers a better understanding of what they are purchasing and increase the likelihood of a sale.

Another important factor is having detailed product descriptions that provide customers with all the information they need to make an informed purchase. Your descriptions should include details about the product's features, benefits, and specifications. You can also include customer reviews and ratings to further build trust and credibility.

Finally, it's important to have a streamlined checkout process. This means minimizing the number of steps required to complete a purchase and offering multiple payment options to make the process as easy as possible for your customers. You can also offer incentives such as free shipping or a discount code for first-time customers to encourage them to complete their purchases. By optimizing your website for conversions, you can improve your sales and grow your dropshipping business.

6. Test and refine your marketing strategy:

Once your dropshipping website is up and running, the next step is to drive traffic to it. There are various marketing channels and strategies that you can use to attract potential customers. One of the most effective ways to do this is through social media. With platforms like Facebook, Instagram, and Twitter, you can reach a large audience and engage with them directly.

Another important aspect of marketing your dropshipping business is search engine optimization (SEO). This involves optimizing your website and content to rank higher in search engine results pages (SERPs). By targeting specific keywords and phrases, you can increase your visibility and attract more organic traffic to your website.

Paid advertising is also a powerful tool for driving traffic to your website. Platforms like Google Ads and Facebook Ads allow you to create targeted campaigns that reach your ideal audience. By setting specific budgets and targeting options, you can maximize your return on investment (ROI) and drive more sales.

It's important to note that not all marketing strategies will work equally well for every business. That's why it's essential to test and refine your approach over time. By tracking your results and analyzing your metrics, you can identify which strategies are most effective for your dropshipping business and make adjustments accordingly.

Some key metrics to track include website traffic, conversion rates, cost per acquisition (CPA), and customer lifetime value (CLV). By monitoring these metrics, you can gain valuable insights into how your marketing efforts are impacting your business and adjust your strategy accordingly.

In addition to testing and refining your marketing strategy, it's also important to stay up-to-date with the latest trends and best practices in the industry. By attending conferences, reading industry blogs and publications, and networking with other dropshippers, you can stay ahead of the curve and position your business for long-term success.

7. Scale your dropshipping business:

Once your dropshipping business is up and running, it's time to focus on scaling it to increase your sales and revenue. Scaling a dropshipping business means expanding the product range, exploring new marketing channels, and optimizing operations to handle a larger volume of orders. Here are some tips on how to scale your dropshipping business:

- **Add more products:**
  Expanding your product range can help you reach a wider audience and increase your revenue. Look for products that complement your existing products or that cater to a new niche within your market. It's important to choose products with a high-profit margin and strong demand to ensure that you are making a profit.

- **Explore new marketing channels:**
  While social media, SEO, and paid advertising are effective ways to drive traffic to your website, there are other marketing channels that you can explore to expand your reach. For example, influencer marketing, email marketing, and affiliate marketing can all be effective ways to reach new customers and generate sales.

- **Optimize operations:**
  As you scale your dropshipping business, it's important to streamline your operations to handle a larger volume of orders. Consider outsourcing tasks like customer service and order fulfillment to a third-party provider to free up your time and resources. You can also use software tools to automate certain tasks, such as order processing and tracking.

- **Monitor your metrics:**
  As you scale your business, it's important to keep track of key metrics like conversion rate, average order value, and customer acquisition cost. These metrics will help you identify areas for improvement and measure the success of

your scaling efforts. Use analytics tools like Google Analytics to track your metrics and make data-driven decisions.

- **Stay customer-focused:**
  While it's important to focus on growth and expansion, it's also important to prioritize your customers. Make sure that you are providing excellent customer service and delivering high-quality products. Encourage customer feedback and use it to improve your products and services. Happy customers are more likely to return and refer others to your business, which can help fuel your growth.

In conclusion, scaling a dropshipping business takes time, effort, and careful planning. By adding more products, exploring new marketing channels, optimizing operations, monitoring metrics, and staying customer-focused, you can successfully scale your dropshipping business and achieve long-term success.

Chapter 8: Offer Consulting Services

Offering consulting services can be a rewarding career path for individuals with expertise in a particular industry or field. Whether you're an experienced professional looking to transition into consulting or a freelancer looking to expand your services, there are several steps you can take to build a successful consulting business. From identifying your niche to developing a pricing strategy and growing your reputation, this chapter will provide insights and tips for anyone interested in offering consulting services.

1. Identifying your consulting niche:

Identifying your consulting niche is crucial in starting your consulting services. Your niche is your area of expertise and the specific industry or market you will serve. By focusing on a niche, you can establish yourself as an expert in that area and tailor your services to the needs of that specific market.

To determine your niche, assess your skills, experience, and expertise. Identify the areas where you excel and have a deep understanding of the industry or market. Consider your education, work experience, and any certifications or licenses you may have. This will help you determine the specific consulting services you can offer.

Once you have identified your niche, research the industry or market to gain a deeper understanding of their needs and pain points. This will allow you to tailor your services to meet those specific needs and stand out from your competitors. Focusing on a niche also allows you to establish a clear and concise marketing message, making it easier to target your ideal clients.

Overall, identifying your consulting niche is the foundation of your consulting business. It sets the stage for the services you offer, your marketing message, and your target audience. By choosing a niche that aligns with your skills and expertise, you can establish yourself as an authority in that area and attract clients who value your unique perspective and insights.

2. Building a website that showcases your consulting services:

Building a website that showcases your consulting services is crucial to your success as a consultant. Your website is often the first point of contact between you and potential clients, and it serves as a platform to showcase your expertise, services, and value proposition. The website should be well-designed, user-friendly, and communicate your brand and message.

To build a website that effectively showcases your consulting services, you should first start by identifying the key elements that should be included. These elements may include a homepage that introduces your services and establishes your brand, an about page that provides information about your background and experience, a services page that outlines the services you offer, a portfolio page that showcases your past work and case studies, and a contact page that allows potential clients to get in touch with you.

It's also important to make sure that your website is visually appealing and easy to navigate. Use

high-quality images and graphics that are relevant
to your consulting niche and make sure your
website is optimized for different devices, such as
desktops, laptops, tablets, and smartphones.
Additionally, your website should be designed in
a way that encourages visitors to take action,
whether it's contacting you for more information,
subscribing to your newsletter, or scheduling a
consultation.

Finally, be sure to include testimonials and case
studies that demonstrate your expertise and the
value you provide to your clients. Testimonials
and case studies can help establish trust with
potential clients and showcase your ability to
deliver results. Overall, building a website that
effectively showcases your consulting services
requires careful planning, attention to detail, and a
focus on delivering value to your target audience.

3. Developing a pricing strategy:

Developing a pricing strategy for your consulting
services is crucial for the success of your business.
There are various pricing models you can use,
such as hourly rates, project-based fees, or

packaged services. You should choose a model that aligns with your niche, experience, and market demand.

If you are just starting, hourly rates may be the best option as they allow you to charge for the time you spend working with a client. However, as you gain experience and expand your services, project-based fees or packaged services may be more appropriate. These pricing models provide a clear scope of work and pricing for clients, allowing them to budget accordingly.

It's also important to consider your competition when setting your rates. Research what other consultants in your niche charge for their services and make sure your prices are competitive. However, don't undervalue yourself. It's essential to price your services based on the value you provide to clients, rather than trying to undercut competitors.

When communicating your pricing to potential clients, it's essential to be transparent and clear. Provide a breakdown of your fees and what clients can expect to receive for their investment. This will help build trust with clients and ensure they understand the value of your services. It's also important to communicate any additional costs, such as expenses or materials, upfront to avoid any surprises for clients.

In conclusion, developing a pricing strategy for your consulting services requires careful consideration of your niche, experience, and market demand. Choosing the right pricing model and setting competitive rates will help attract and retain clients. Being transparent and clear about your fees and the value you provide is essential for building trust and credibility with potential clients.

4. Growing your consulting business:

Growing a consulting business takes time, effort, and a strategic approach. One of the most effective ways to grow your consulting business is by establishing yourself as an authority in your niche. To do this, you need to build a strong reputation by consistently delivering high-quality services, generating positive feedback from clients, and publishing content that demonstrates your expertise.

Networking is another important aspect of growing your consulting business. Attending conferences, industry events, and other professional gatherings can provide valuable opportunities to connect with potential clients and other professionals in your field. Networking can also help you stay up-to-date with the latest industry trends and best practices, which is essential for delivering top-notch services to your clients.

In addition to networking, publishing thought leadership content is a powerful way to establish yourself as an authority in your niche. This could include writing blog posts, creating videos, or publishing white papers that demonstrate your expertise and provide valuable insights to potential clients. By sharing your knowledge and expertise, you can position yourself as a go-to expert in your industry and attract more clients to your consulting business.

Leveraging social media is also an effective way to grow your consulting business. Platforms like LinkedIn, Twitter, and Facebook can provide valuable opportunities to connect with potential clients and showcase your services. By creating and sharing engaging content, you can build a following on social media and generate leads for your consulting business.

Finally, investing in your own education and skill development is crucial for staying competitive in the consulting industry. Whether it's attending conferences and workshops, enrolling in online courses, or earning advanced certifications, investing in your own education and skill development can help you stay on top of industry trends and best practices, and deliver the highest quality services to your clients. It also demonstrates to potential clients that you are committed to providing the best possible service and continually improving your skills and knowledge.

Chapter 9: Freelance Services

As the world of work continues to evolve, more and more people are turning to freelance services as a means of earning a living. Whether you're looking to escape the nine-to-five grind, gain more control over your work schedule, or pursue your passions on your terms, freelancing can offer a variety of benefits. However, to succeed in this competitive market, it's important to understand the key components of a successful freelance business. In this chapter, we'll explore some of the essential steps you can take to identify your in-demand skills, build a strong portfolio, find clients, and maximize your earnings as a freelancer.

1. Identifying in-demand skills:

Identifying in-demand skills is a crucial step in building a successful freelance career. It's important to stay up-to-date with the latest trends and technologies in your industry to ensure you offer the skills that are in high demand. Market research can help you understand what clients are looking for in a freelancer and what services they are willing to pay for. Freelancers can also turn to job boards to see what types of projects are currently in demand.

Networking with other professionals in your field is another effective way to identify in-demand skills. By attending industry events, conferences, and webinars, you can connect with other freelancers and learn about their areas of expertise. You can also join online communities and social media groups that are specific to your industry. These platforms provide an opportunity to connect with other professionals, share knowledge, and stay informed about industry trends.

Identifying in-demand skills also requires a deep understanding of your strengths and capabilities. As a freelancer, you should assess your skills, experience, and expertise to determine what sets you apart from other professionals in your field. This self-assessment can help you identify areas where you can specialize and differentiate yourself in a crowded market.

Moreover, looking at job postings can also help you identify in-demand skills. Reviewing job postings on freelancing platforms and job boards can provide insight into the types of skills that clients are looking for in freelancers. By examining the job requirements and qualifications, you can identify the specific skills and expertise that are in demand in your industry.

In conclusion, identifying in-demand skills is a critical step in building a successful freelance career. It involves conducting market research, networking with other professionals, and assessing your skills and expertise. By understanding what clients are looking for in a freelancer, you can develop the skills and services that are in high demand and differentiate yourself in a crowded market.

Some of the most in-demand skills for freelancers include:

- Writing and Editing
- Graphic design
- Web development and design
- Social media management

- Search engine optimization (SEO)
- Video editing and production
- Virtual assistance
- Translation and localization
- Online advertising and marketing
- Project management

2. Creating a portfolio:

Creating a portfolio is an essential step for any freelancer looking to attract potential clients. It provides a platform to showcase your skills, experience, and past work to potential clients. Your portfolio is a reflection of your brand, and it is important to ensure that it is professional, visually appealing, and easy to navigate.

The first step in creating a portfolio is to determine what to include. The portfolio should highlight your most impressive work, so it's important to carefully select the examples that best demonstrate your skills and experience. You may want to include a range of projects that showcase your versatility, as well as any specialized expertise you may have.

Testimonials and reviews from satisfied clients can also be powerful tools for building trust with potential clients. Including a section of client testimonials in your portfolio can help showcase your ability to deliver results and provide exceptional service. It's important to ask for testimonials from clients and to include them in your portfolio with their permission.

In addition to showcasing your work and client testimonials, your portfolio should also provide information about your skills, experience, and expertise. A brief introduction about yourself and your background can help potential clients get to know you and understand why you are the right person for the job.

When it comes to presenting your portfolio, it's important to choose a platform that is easy to navigate and visually appealing. There are many website builders and hosting platforms available that allow you to create a professional-looking portfolio without any technical skills. You may also consider using social media platforms like LinkedIn or Instagram to showcase your work and reach potential clients.

Finally, it's important to keep your portfolio up-to-date with your latest work and projects. As you continue to grow and develop your skills as a freelancer, be sure to update your portfolio to reflect your latest accomplishments and showcase your ongoing growth and expertise.

In summary, creating a portfolio is a crucial step for any freelancer looking to attract potential clients. By showcasing your skills, experience, and past work in a professional and visually appealing way, you can demonstrate your expertise and stand out in a crowded freelance market.

3. Finding clients:

Finding clients is a crucial aspect of freelancing. Without a steady stream of clients, a freelancer's income can quickly dry up, making it challenging to sustain their business. There are several ways to find clients, including networking with other professionals in your industry, joining freelance job boards and websites, reaching out to potential clients directly, asking for referrals from past clients, and utilizing social media.

Networking with other professionals in your industry is a great way to find clients. By attending industry events and joining professional organizations, you can meet other professionals in your field and build relationships with them. You can also share your work and services with potential clients who may be interested in hiring you for their projects. Networking is all about building relationships, so make sure to attend events and engage with other professionals.

Joining freelance job boards and websites is another way to find clients. Many clients post their projects on these platforms, allowing freelancers to apply for them. These job boards and websites also offer the opportunity to create a profile that showcases your skills, experience, and portfolio, making it easier for clients to find and hire you. Some popular job boards and websites for freelancers include Upwork, Freelancer, and Fiverr.

Reaching out to potential clients directly is another effective way to find clients. You can use online directories, such as LinkedIn or Crunchbase, to find potential clients who may be interested in your services. Once you identify potential clients, you can reach out to them directly via email or social media to introduce yourself and offer your services.

Asking for referrals from past clients can also help you find new clients. Satisfied clients are often happy to recommend freelancers they have worked with in the past to their contacts. Make sure to maintain positive relationships with your clients and ask for referrals when the project is completed.

Lastly, utilizing social media is a great way to showcase your work and reach potential clients. By creating profiles on popular social media platforms such as Twitter, Facebook, and Instagram, you can share your portfolio, promote your services, and connect with potential clients who may be interested in hiring you. You can also use social media to engage with your followers and establish yourself as an expert in your field.

4. Maximizing your earnings as a freelancer:

To maximize your earnings as a freelancer, it's important to set clear pricing and payment terms with your clients. You should also focus on building long-term relationships with your clients, as repeat business can be a significant source of income. Additionally, consider diversifying your income streams by offering additional services or creating digital products related to your freelance work.

Chapter 10: Investing in Stocks and Crypto

Investing in stocks and cryptocurrency can be an exciting and potentially lucrative way to generate passive income. However, it's important to approach these markets with caution and a clear understanding of the risks involved. As with any investment, there is no guarantee of success, but by developing a sound investment strategy and staying informed on market trends, it is possible to maximize your earnings and build long-term wealth. Whether you're looking to invest in dividend-paying stocks for a regular source of income or take a more speculative approach with growth stocks or cryptocurrencies, there are a variety of strategies to consider.

With careful research and a disciplined approach, investing in stocks and crypto can be a valuable addition to your overall investment portfolio.

1. **Understanding the stock and crypto markets:**

Investing in stocks and crypto can be an exciting and potentially profitable venture, but it's crucial to first understand the workings of the markets. Understanding market capitalization, for example, is important in determining the value of a company's outstanding shares. It's calculated by multiplying the number of shares outstanding by the current market price per share, and it helps investors determine a company's size and potential growth.

Volatility is another important concept to grasp before investing in stocks or crypto. It refers to the degree of variation of a stock or cryptocurrency's price over time, and it's influenced by factors like economic news, geopolitical events, and investor sentiment. Understanding volatility is key in managing risk, as it can indicate potential price swings and allow investors to make informed decisions on when to buy or sell.

Risk management is also an important component of understanding the stock and crypto markets. All investments carry some level of risk, but it's important to understand the specific risks associated with different types of investments. For example, stocks can be subject to company-specific risks, such as a decline in sales or the departure of key executives, as well as broader market risks, such as changes in interest rates or inflation.

Keeping up-to-date on news and trends in the markets is also essential in making informed investment decisions. Factors such as economic data, corporate earnings reports, and political events can all impact the stock and crypto markets. By staying informed, investors can adjust their investment strategies accordingly and capitalize on potential opportunities or minimize risks.

In summary, understanding the stock and crypto markets requires a solid grasp of market capitalization, volatility, risk management, and staying informed on news and trends. By familiarizing themselves with these concepts, investors can make more informed decisions and potentially increase their chances of success in the markets.

2. Developing a sound investment strategy:

Developing a sound investment strategy is crucial to maximizing your earnings and minimizing your risk in the stock and crypto markets. The first step is setting clear investment goals, which may include long-term wealth accumulation or short-term income generation. These goals will guide your investment decisions and help you stay focused on achieving your desired outcomes.

Once you have set your investment goals, the next step is to decide on an asset allocation that aligns with your risk tolerance and investment goals. This involves determining what percentage of your portfolio you will allocate to different types of assets, such as stocks, bonds, and cryptocurrencies. A general rule of thumb is to invest in a mix of assets to spread out risk and maximize potential returns.

Diversification is another critical aspect of a sound investment strategy. By investing in a mix of assets, you can spread out risk and reduce the impact of market volatility on your portfolio. This may involve investing in different sectors of the stock market, such as technology or healthcare, or different types of cryptocurrencies, such as Bitcoin and Ethereum.

In addition to diversification, a long-term investment mindset is essential for success in the stock and crypto markets. Trying to time the market or make quick profits can lead to poor investment decisions and significant losses. Instead, focus on investing in quality assets that align with your investment goals and hold them for the long term. Over time, this approach can help you build wealth and generate passive income.

Finally, it's important to regularly review and adjust your investment strategy as needed. As the markets and your investment goals change, you may need to make changes to your asset allocation or investment approach. By staying informed and flexible, you can adapt your investment strategy to meet your changing needs and maximize your earnings over time.

3. Maximizing your earnings through investing:

Investing in dividend-paying stocks is a popular strategy for investors who are seeking regular income from their investments. Dividend stocks are those issued by companies that have a history of paying out dividends to shareholders. Typically, these companies are established, stable, and have a long-term track record of profitability. Dividend stocks can provide investors with a steady stream of income, making them a good choice for those who are looking for a source of passive income.

On the other hand, growth stocks are those issued by companies that are expected to grow at a higher rate than the overall market. These companies typically reinvest their earnings back into the business rather than paying dividends to shareholders. As a result, growth stocks can be more volatile than dividend stocks but offer greater potential for capital appreciation over the long term. Growth stocks can be a good choice for investors who are willing to take on more risk in exchange for potentially higher returns.

Investing in index funds is another way to maximize your earnings through investing. Index funds are passively managed investment funds that track a particular index, such as the S&P 500. Because they are not actively managed, index funds typically have lower fees compared to actively managed funds. Additionally, index funds provide investors with exposure to a wide range of stocks or cryptocurrencies, making them a good choice for those who want to diversify their portfolio and spread out their risk.

Another strategy to maximize earnings through investing is to dollar-cost average. This involves investing a fixed amount of money at regular intervals, regardless of the current market conditions. By investing a fixed amount of money at regular intervals, you can take advantage of dollar-cost averaging, which can help you avoid buying in at a market peak or selling at a market bottom.

There are several strategies you can use to maximize your earnings through investing. It's important to understand the different investment options available to you and choose the strategy that aligns best with your investment goals, risk tolerance, and investment timeline.

Overall, investing in stocks and crypto requires patience, discipline, and a solid understanding of the markets. With the right approach, it can be a rewarding way to generate passive income and build long-term wealth.

Conclusion

In conclusion, this guide has provided a comprehensive overview of various strategies for earning money online, each requiring hard work, dedication, and patience. It is important to remember that success is not achieved overnight, but with consistent effort and motivation, you can see results.

To achieve success in the online world, it is essential to take action and implement the strategies discussed in this guide. Begin with small steps, set realistic goals, and focus on one method at a time. With perseverance and dedication, you can build on your successes and expand your sources of income.

Moreover, it is crucial to stay true to your values and interests and prioritize providing value to your customers or audience. By doing so, you can create a sustainable and fulfilling online business. Whether you are starting or looking to grow your existing business, this guide offers valuable insights and inspiration to support your journey toward financial freedom. So, take the first step today, and with determination and focus, you can achieve your goals and live the life you've always dreamed of.

Ending Note:

It's important to note that this book is solely intended for educational purposes and is not a guarantee of success. While the strategies and techniques discussed in this book have been proven effective, individual results may vary. It's crucial to understand that achieving financial success requires hard work and dedication. There may be obstacles and setbacks along the way, but it's important to stay motivated and persevere. Remember that this book is a starting point, and it's up to you to take action and implement the strategies discussed to achieve your goals. Always be open to learning and adapting your approach as you go along. With the right mindset and a commitment to continual growth and improvement, you can turn the knowledge gained from this book into tangible results.

www.ingramcontent.com/pod-product-compliance
Lightning Source LLC
Chambersburg PA
CBHW070553220526
45467CB00003B/1201